SALADS

Simple & Delicious
SALADS

Katharine Blakemore

APPLE

Contents

Introducing Salads

A salad is a mixture of raw or cooked foods which are seasoned, and usually served with a dressing. It's one of the most versatile of dishes as it can be served as a first course, accompany a principal dish, or be a main course in its own right. Substantial meat or fish salads or an interesting mixture of these dishes can make a magnificent focal point to a meal.

Made with the freshest and most nutritious ingredients, salads have many advantages, besides the vitamin—and protein—rich foods that go into them. They can contain entirely raw components, so no special skills are required from the cook and none of the goodness is taken from the food by heating. It is very important when buying food for salads, especially those made from raw vegetables and fruit, that only the freshest and best quality ingredients are used.

Most salads can be prepared in advance, which is very useful when entertaining, and others can be assembled in a matter of minutes. For salad making, no specialized equipment is required apart from a chopping board, a sharp knife and a large mixing bowl, although a salad spinner for rinsing and drying green leaf vegetables is a handy aid.

Dressings are considered essential to most salads and there is a wide variety of the traditional ingredients—oil and vinegar—to choose from. Extra virgin olive oil is the best quality olive oil but light sunflower or vegetable oils are popular, and good grapeseed, sesame and nut oils are available.

There are fine wine, fruit, sherry and herb vinegars on the market and many different mustards and peppers, so experiment with different combinations. Other dressings are based on mayonnaise or yogurt.

It is not necessary to stick rigidly to each recipe. If an ingredient is not available, or not to your taste, substitute another and be inventive. Above all, whatever the combination, a salad should be a bright and nutritious dish.

NOTE All recipes require fresh herbs and greens unless specified.

Green Leaves

Mesclun salad with pesto

Serves 4 as a side dish

FOR PESTO
½ cup (¾ oz/25 g) well-packed basil leaves
½ cup (¾ oz/25 g) well-packed chopped arugula (rocket) leaves
½ cup (2 oz/60 g) pine nuts, toasted
2 cloves garlic, chopped
pinch sea salt
½ cup (2 oz/60 g) freshly grated Parmesan cheese
juice of 1 lemon
½ cup (4 fl oz/125 ml) extra virgin olive oil

FOR SALAD
2 ripe avocados
juice of 1 lemon
2 tablespoons balsamic vinegar
2 tablespoons extra virgin olive oil
4 cups (4 oz/125 g) loosely packed mixed fresh salad leaves (mesclun)

To make pesto: Place basil, arugula, pine nuts, garlic, salt, Parmesan and lemon juice in a food processor. Process until well blended, about 15 seconds. With food processor running, gradually add oil. Process until mixture has consistency of thick paste. Use a little less or a little more oil if necessary, to achieve right consistency. Spoon pesto into a screw-top jar and refrigerate until ready to use.

To make salad: Slice each avocado in half through stem, and remove pit and skin. Cut into 1-inch (2.5-cm) cubes and place in a bowl. Add lemon juice and gently toss avocados in juice. Add 3 tablespoons pesto to bowl and gently toss avocados until coated. (Store remaining pesto in refrigerator, and use for salads, pasta, sandwiches and sauces.)

In a small bowl, combine balsamic vinegar and olive oil.

Place salad leaves in a serving bowl and drizzle with vinegar and oil. Add pesto avocado, toss and serve immediately.

Green salad

Serves 4
4–6 cups (4–6 oz/125–180 g) mixed fresh salad leaves
1 small red onion
1 tablespoon fresh or ½ teaspoon dried herb,
e.g. basil, thyme, tarragon, chives, mint
Vinaigrette or choice of dressing (see pages 60–61)

Tear salad leaves into bite-size pieces and place in a salad bowl. Peel onion, slice thinly and separate into rings. Scatter onion and herbs over salad and mix lightly to combine. Pour dressing over salad, toss lightly and serve immediately.

NOTE Choose an interesting mix of salad lettuces and leaves for color, flavor and texture. Add blanched and refreshed snow peas (mange-tout) for extra interest.

Table greens

Serves 4–6
fresh herbs of choice
leaves from 1–2 heads butter (Boston) lettuce
leaves from 1 red or green leaf lettuce (oak leaf, Lollo Rossa or coral)
2 cups (4 oz/125 g) bean sprouts, rinsed and drained
½ cucumber, seeded and thinly sliced

Trim herb stems and rinse leaves. Keep sprigs whole. Clean lettuce leaves. Rinse sprouts, and remove "tails" if desired. Prepare cucumber.

To serve, arrange lettuce leaves and herbs to one side of a large bowl or platter, and place sprouts and cucumber on the other side.

NOTE For a Vietnamese-style salad (Rau song/Rau thom), choose herbs such as sprigs of cilantro (fresh coriander) (rau mui/rau ngo), peppermint and spearmint (rau baa ha/rau huong lui), Vietnamese mint (rau ram), perilla (rau tia to), Vietnamese lemon balm (rau kinh gioi), eryngo (sawtooth coriander/rau mui tau/rau ngo gai), piper leaf (bo la lot), and sweet Thai basil (rau hung que).

Bitter greens salad

Serves 4

2 firm, ripe pears such as Beurre Bosc, unpeeled
¼ cup (2 fl oz/60 ml) extra virgin olive oil
freshly ground black pepper
1 tablespoon smooth or mild mustard, such as Dijon
1 teaspoon white wine or sherry vinegar
sea salt
3 Asian pears (nashi), unpeeled
4 cups (4 oz/125 g) mixed bitter salad leaves such as Belgian endive,
radicchio and baby curly endive
½ cup (2 oz/60 g) coarsely chopped walnuts
½ cup (½ oz/15 g) chervil sprigs (optional)

Wash and dry pears, then slice as thinly as possible using a Japanese vegetable slicer or mandoline. Slice each pear with blossom end facing base of slicer and stem facing top. Slice down to core, then turn pear over and slice other side down to core. Ideally each slice will be fringed with skin.

Spread out pear slices on a dehydrator sheet or nonstick baking sheet. Brush slices lightly with 1 tablespoon olive oil and sprinkle with a tiny amount of pepper. Dry pears, either in a dehydrator or oven set to 110°F (55°C/Gas ¼) for 2–4 hours until frilly at the edges and crisp. Remove from dehydrator or oven and cool.

In a bowl, place mustard and vinegar and whisk in remaining olive oil. Season to taste with salt and pepper.

Cut Asian pears into quarters, remove cores, then cut into even-sized chunks. Toss through dressing to coat.

Choose small salad leaves or slice larger ones finely and toss with Asian pears. Add walnuts then transfer to serving plates and garnish with chervil if using. Place a pile of dried pear crisps on top of each salad.

Vegetables

Carrot, romaine and feta salad

Serves 4

4 medium carrots, peeled

1 head baby romaine (cos) lettuce or ½ head normal-sized romaine (cos) lettuce

¾ cup (4 oz /125 g) firm feta cheese, cut into ½-inch (12-mm) cubes

¼ cup (¼ oz/7 g) fresh dill, chopped

FOR DRESSING

3 tablespoons lemon juice

2 tablespoons olive oil

¼ teaspoon sea salt

freshly ground black pepper to taste

Cut carrots in half lengthwise. Using a vegetable peeler, slice carrots into thin long strips.

Place carrot strips in a bowl of ice water and place in refrigerator until carrot curls, about 15 minutes. Drain carrots and pat dry with paper towels.

Slice lettuce into 1-inch (2.5-cm) shreds. Combine carrots, lettuce, feta cheese and dill in a serving bowl.

To make dressing: Combine lemon juice, olive oil, and salt and pepper in a screw-top jar and shake well to mix.

Pour dressing over salad and toss until well combined. Serve chilled.

Rainbow bell pepper salad

Serves 4–6

1½ tablespoons red wine vinegar

2 shallots (French shallots), finely
sliced

2 cloves garlic, crushed

½ cup (3½ oz/110 g) peeled, seeded
and diced tomato

2 tablespoons nonpareil (baby) capers,
rinsed and chopped

¼ teaspoon cayenne pepper

1 tablespoon chopped preserved lemon

⅓ cup (3 fl oz/90 ml) extra virgin
olive oil

sea salt

freshly ground black pepper

2 yellow or orange bell peppers
(capsicums), seeded and very finely
sliced lengthwise

2 red bell peppers (capsicums), seeded
and very finely sliced lengthwise

1 green bell pepper (capsicum), seeded
and very finely sliced lengthwise

⅓ cup (⅓ oz/10 g) finely sliced flat-leaf
(Italian) parsley leaves

In a large bowl, stir together vinegar,
shallot, garlic, tomato, capers,
cayenne pepper and preserved lemon.
Whisk in olive oil and season to taste
with salt and pepper. Add finely
sliced bell pepper and toss through.
Cover and set aside for 20 minutes or
so, tossing occasionally. After this
time bell pepper will have begun to
soften slightly and juices will mingle.
Check seasoning, add parsley, and
transfer to serving plates.

NOTE Preserved lemons are widely
available at delicatessens and Middle
Eastern stores.

Grilled pepper salad

Serves 4–6
2 large red bell peppers (capsicums)
2 large green bell peppers (capsicums)
2 large yellow bell peppers (capsicums)
3 tablespoons olive oil
1 clove garlic, crushed
salt and freshly ground black pepper

Cut bell peppers into quarters and discard seeds. Lay on a baking sheet skin side up.

Broil (grill) until skin begins to turn brown and blister. Remove from heat, let stand until cool enough to handle, then peel off skin.

Cut each piece of bell pepper in half again. Arrange in a shallow dish. Mix olive oil with garlic, salt and pepper. Pour over bell peppers.

NOTE These bell peppers can be prepared up to 1 day in advance. Keep covered in the refrigerator but bring to room temperature to serve.

Yellow bell peppers can be omitted and replaced with some sliced yellow tomatoes when available.

Asian coconut and vegetable salad

Serves 4

1 cup (8 fl oz/250 ml) water

½ cup (2 oz/60 g) unsweetened dried (desiccated) shredded coconut

1 teaspoon shrimp paste

1 teaspoon chili powder or to taste

1 clove garlic, finely chopped

½ teaspoon brown sugar

2 tablespoons fresh lime juice

2 cups (2½ oz/75 g) watercress

1 carrot, peeled and julienned

8 small red radishes, trimmed and julienned

½ English (hothouse) cucumber, peeled, seeded and thinly sliced

1 cup (4 oz/125 g) bean sprouts

4 scallions (shallots/spring onions), sliced

2 kaffir lime leaves, finely shredded or

½ teaspoon grated lime zest

Combine water, coconut, shrimp paste, chili powder, garlic and sugar in a small saucepan. Place over medium heat, stir until mixture boils and then cook for 3 minutes.

Remove from heat and allow to cool completely. Stir in lime juice. Chill coconut mixture until ready to serve.

In a large bowl, combine watercress, carrot, radishes, cucumber, bean sprouts, scallions and lime leaves. Toss until well combined. Add coconut mixture and toss again. Serve immediately.

Simple potato salad

Serves 6–8
2 lb (1 kg) small new potatoes
Vinaigrette Dressing (see page 60)
2 celery stalks
4 scallions (shallots/spring onions)
1 cup (8 fl oz/250 ml) of purchased or homemade Mayonnaise (see page 61)
½ cup (4 fl oz/125 ml) sour cream
1½ teaspoons Dijon mustard or horseradish cream
freshly ground black pepper
chopped parsley, for serving

Place potatoes in a saucepan of lightly salted water to cover, bring to a boil and cook until just tender, 10–12 minutes. Drain and cool until easy to handle. Peel, if desired, and cut into thick pieces.

Place warm potatoes in a bowl, drizzle with vinaigrette and toss lightly to coat. Cover and refrigerate until cold, about 1–2 hours.

Trim and slice celery and scallions and add to potatoes.

Combine mayonnaise, sour cream and mustard in a bowl. Season to taste with pepper. Lightly fold mixture through potatoes. Refrigerate until required. Serve well chilled, sprinkled with parsley.

Salade paysanne

Serves 4–6

4 oz (125 g) fine green (French) beans
salt
1 lb (500 g) small new potatoes,
  cooked in their skins and cooled
4 tomatoes, cut into wedges
2 pickled cucumbers, chopped
1 small onion, finely chopped
1 clove garlic, crushed
3 tablespoons Mayonnaise (see page
  61)
1 tablespoon white wine vinegar
freshly ground black pepper

3 hard-cooked (boiled) eggs, quartered
1 tablespoon chopped fresh parsley

Cook beans in lightly salted water for 5 minutes. Drain and cool.

Place beans in a salad bowl with potatoes, tomatoes and pickled cucumbers.

Combine onion, garlic, mayonnaise, vinegar and black pepper. Add to bowl and mix well.

Arrange eggs on top of salad, then sprinkle with chopped parsley.

Asparagus salad

Serves 4–6

1 lb (500 g) fresh asparagus spears
1 tablespoon olive oil
2 teaspoons walnut or hazelnut oil
2 teaspoons red wine vinegar or sherry
  vinegar
1 cup (4 oz/125 g) shaved Parmesan
  cheese
sea salt and black pepper to taste

Trim off woody stems from asparagus. Wash asparagus well. Bring a medium saucepan of water to a boil. Add asparagus, boil for 30 seconds and remove.

Drizzle asparagus with olive oil and grill (broil) on high heat for 1 minute.

Arrange asparagus on a plate. Top with a drizzle of walnut or hazelnut oil and a splash of vinegar. Sprinkle with Parmesan shavings and season with sea salt and pepper to taste.

VARIATION If you do not wish to grill the asparagus, cook asparagus in a large pot of boiling salted water until crisp-tender, about 3–6 minutes. Drain; rinse with cold water and drain again. Drizzle with oil and vinegar and top with shaved Parmesan cheese.

Baby beet salad with aioli

Serves 4–6

4 bunches baby beets (beetroots), red and golden if possible
2 handfuls baby beet (beetroot) leaves
½ red onion, chopped
sea salt and freshly ground black pepper
olive oil, for drizzling

FOR AIOLI
6 cloves garlic, crushed
3 egg yolks
pinch salt
1 teaspoon Dijon mustard
2 teaspoons lemon juice
1¼ cups (10 fl oz/300 ml) olive oil
white pepper to taste

Cut off beet tops, leaving 2 inches (5 cm) of stem. Reserve leaves. Scrub beets with a soft brush. Bring a saucepan of water to a boil. Add beets, reduce heat, cover and simmer beets until tender, about 20 minutes. Remove from heat and let beets cool in liquid. When beets are cool enough to handle, slip off skins and trim stems. Refrigerate until ready to serve.

To make aioli: Place garlic, egg yolks, salt and mustard in a food processor and process until just combined, about 10 seconds. With the motor still running, add lemon juice, then add oil very slowly, in drops from a teaspoon. As mixture thickens, increase flow of oil, so it becomes a steady stream. Taste and add white pepper and a little more lemon juice if desired. (If mixture becomes too thick, blend in 1 tablespoon hot water just before serving.) Spoon aioli into 4 small bowls and refrigerate until ready to serve.

Arrange beet leaves on serving plates and top with cooked baby beets. Sprinkle beets with chopped onion and salt and pepper, and drizzle liberally with olive oil. Serve with chilled aioli.

Coleslaw

Seves 6–8

1 small head green cabbage, cored and sliced as thinly as possible
1 small head red cabbage, cored and sliced as thinly as possible
4 celery stalks, finely chopped
4 scallions (shallots/spring onions), green and white parts, finely chopped
4 carrots, shredded
1 cup (8 fl oz/250 ml) Mayonnaise (see page 61)
3 tablespoons fresh lemon juice
salt and freshly ground black pepper to taste

Combine cabbage, celery, scallions and carrots in a large bowl. Mix together mayonnaise, lemon juice, salt and pepper in a separate bowl and pour over cabbage mixture. Toss to combine well and refrigerate for at least 1 hour before serving.

NOTE Before making coleslaw, place cabbage in a large bowl and cover with ice water; refrigerate for 1 hour and drain thoroughly.

Add 2 tablespoons caraway seeds to the mayonnaise, if desired.

Red and green cabbage and kale coleslaw

Serves 4

½ cup (2 oz/60 g) pine nuts
½ cup (2½ oz/75 g) macadamia nuts
1 clove garlic, crushed
1 small inner celery stalk, chopped
¼ cup (2 fl oz/60 ml) lemon juice
¼ cup (2 fl oz/60 ml) water
sea salt
freshly ground black pepper
½ cup (4 fl oz/125 ml) extra virgin olive oil

2⅔ cups (8 oz/250 g) very finely shredded Savoy cabbage
2 cups (6 oz/180 g) very finely shredded red cabbage
1 cup (3 oz/90 g) very finely shredded kale
4 medium carrots, coarsely grated
½ cup (½ oz/15 g) chopped fresh herbs

In a blender, place nuts, garlic, celery, lemon juice and water with a pinch each of salt and pepper. Add half the oil and blend until very smooth. Check seasoning.

Place shredded cabbage and kale in a large bowl and mix together with carrot, then add dressing and stir well for 2 minutes to ensure vegetables are well coated. Cover and set aside for 1 hour or so, tossing occasionally, until cabbage begins to soften slightly.

When ready to serve, stir in remaining olive oil along with herbs. Check seasoning and serve in a large bowl or individual mounds.

Fruits and Tomatoes

Green papaya salad

Serves 4–6
1 lb (500 g) green papaya, peeled and seeded
3 cloves garlic, peeled
10 fresh small green chilies
2 long (snake) beans, or about 8 green beans, cut into 1-inch (2.5-cm) pieces
2 tablespoons dried shrimp
2 tablespoons fish sauce
2 tablespoons fresh lime juice
1 teaspoon palm sugar
1 tablespoon anchovy paste (optional)
1 firm tomato, coarsely chopped, or 5 cherry tomatoes, halved
2 tablespoons coarsely ground roasted peanuts

Using a knife or shredder, shred papaya into long, thin strips. You should have about 3 cups (10–12 oz/300–375 g); set aside.

In a large mortar or bowl, combine garlic, chilies, and beans, and pound to coarsely bruise with a pestle. Add papaya and pound again to just bruise ingredients.

Add dried shrimp, fish sauce, lime juice and palm sugar. Stir together until sugar has dissolved. Add anchovy paste, if using, and tomato. Gently pound to combine flavors.

Transfer to a serving platter, sprinkle with peanuts and serve.

NOTE If unripe or green papaya is unavailable, substitute with shredded, peeled carrot, cucumber or melon.

Tomato and onion salad

Seves 4

1 red onion, sliced thinly
½ teaspoon salt
½ teaspoon paprika (optional)
2 ripe tomatoes, thinly sliced
1 tablespoon vinegar

Mix onions with salt and leave in a colander or sieve to drain for 10 minutes; rinse under cold water, drain. Mix with paprika if using. Arrange tomato slices on a serving plate and top with onions. Drizzle with vinegar and serve.

Marinated tomato salad

Serves 2–4

8 basil leaves, chopped
1 clove garlic, finely chopped
4 tablespoons extra virgin olive oil
8 ripe red tomatoes, chopped roughly
2 cups (16 oz/500 g) ricotta cheese or
**   cottage cheese**

Combine basil, garlic and oil. Pour over tomatoes and let stand for up to 1 hour (10 minutes will do).

Pile ricotta on top and serve at room temperature.

NOTE If serving as a salad with bread, add 2 teaspoons balsamic or red wine vinegar to the oil mixture if desired.

Watermelon and tomato salad

Seves 4–6
4 beefsteak tomatoes, thinly sliced
½ watermelon, peeled
1 red onion, finely chopped
1 tablespoon chopped fresh mint
1 tablespoon lemon juice
1 teaspoon sugar
3 tablespoons vegetable oil
salt and freshly ground black pepper
fresh mint sprigs, for garnish

Line a salad bowl with tomato slices.

Cut watermelon into small, even-size pieces, discarding seeds. Arrange over tomatoes, sprinkle with onion.

Combine chopped mint, lemon juice, sugar, oil, salt and pepper. Pour over salad, then garnish with mint sprigs.

NOTE When watermelons are out of season this refreshing salad can be made with a honeydew melon, but omit the sugar in the dressing.

Tomato, basil and bocconcini salad

Serves 4
6 large tomatoes, sliced
virgin olive oil
zest and juice of 1 lemon
4 bocconcini, sliced thinly
fresh basil leaves, torn
black pepper
sea salt

Arrange tomato slices in overlapping circles on a large plate. Drizzle olive oil over tomatoes. Scatter lemon zest over tomatoes with a little lemon juice. Top with slices of bocconcini and torn basil. Grind black pepper and sprinkle on top.

Serve immediately or cover and refrigerate. To serve, grind sea salt over top of tomatoes.

NOTE Slice the tomatoes horizontally. Tear the basil so it doesn't bruise; do not cut it.

Greek salad

Serves 4–5

1 crisp lettuce

4 large tomatoes, cut into wedges

1 cucumber, cut into large cubes

1 red bell pepper (capsicum), seeded and chopped

1 green bell pepper (capsicum), seeded and chopped

1¼ cups (6 oz/180 g) feta cheese, cubed

½ cup (2½ oz/75 g) black olives

1 onion, sliced

FOR DRESSING

4 tablespoons olive oil

2 tablespoons wine vinegar

1 clove garlic, crushed

1 tablespoon chopped fresh marjoram or 1 teaspoon dried marjoram

Tear lettuce into large pieces and place in a salad bowl. Add tomatoes, cucumber and bell peppers. Arrange feta cheese, olives and onion on top.

Place dressing ingredients in a screw-top jar. Shake well then pour over salad.

Village salad

Serves 6

8 romaine (cos) lettuce leaves
small bunch arugula (rocket)
4 medium tomatoes
½ English (hothouse) cucumber
   or 2 Lebanese cucumbers
1 green bell pepper (capsicum), halved,
   cored and seeded
2 medium red onions, sliced
4 oz (125 g) feta cheese, diced
½ cup (2½ oz/75 g) black olives

DRESSING

⅓ cup (3 fl oz/90 ml) extra virgin olive
   oil
1 tablespoon white wine vinegar
2 teaspoons finely chopped fresh
   flat-leaf (Italian) parsley
1 teaspoon finely chopped fresh mint

salt
freshly ground black pepper

Wash lettuce and arugula, dry and tear into pieces. Cut tomatoes into wedges. Peel cucumber and halve lengthwise; then cut crosswise into ½-inch (1-cm) slices. Cut bell pepper into thick strips. Separate onion slices into rings.

To make dressing: Combine oil, vinegar, parsley and mint in a small bowl. Whisk together, then add salt and pepper to taste.

Place lettuce, arugula, tomatoes, cucumbers, bell peppers and onions in a bowl. Top with feta cheese and olives. Pour on dressing just before serving and toss.

Tomato salad

Serves 4

6 medium tomatoes, peeled
6 tablespoons chopped fresh cilantro
   (fresh coriander)
1 small hot chili, or freshly ground
   black pepper
juice of ½ lemon
about 1 teaspoon salt
¼ cup (2 fl oz/60 ml) olive oil

Slice tomatoes into a bowl and sprinkle layers with cilantro. If using chili, cut off stem, slit open and remove seeds; then finely chop.

In a small bowl, combine chopped chili or ground pepper with lemon juice and salt. Beat in olive oil. Pour dressing over tomatoes and let stand for 15 minutes before serving.

Red and white cabbage salad with banana

Serves 4–6

2 cups (8 oz/250 g) shredded red
   cabbage
2 cups (8 oz/250 g) shredded Dutch
   white cabbage
2 large firm bananas
1 tablespoon lemon juice
1 cup (3 oz/90 g) toasted flaked
   (desiccated) coconut
3 tablespoons Mayonnaise (see page 61)
salt and freshly ground black pepper

Place shredded cabbage in a salad bowl. Thinly slice bananas, brush with lemon juice, and add to bowl with coconut. Stir in mayonnaise, salt and pepper and mix well.

NOTE If only over-ripe bananas are available, mash them with the lemon juice and add them to the salad with the mayonnaise.

Pear and blue cheese salad

Seves 4

1 bunch watercress
4 ripe pears, peeled and cored
⅓ cup (3 oz/90 g) creamy blue cheese
2 tablespoons plain (natural)
   Greek-style yogurt
1 tablespoon vegetable oil
freshly ground black pepper
1 bunch scallions (shallots/spring
   onions), chopped

Line a round serving plate with watercress. Slice pears and arrange in overlapping slices over watercress.

Crumble blue cheese into yogurt, add oil and pepper. Beat well then pour over pears.

Sprinkle with scallions and serve immediately.

NOTE This salad can be prepared 2–3 hours in advance, but brush the pear slices with lemon juice to prevent them from going brown.

Suitable cheeses for this salad are Dolcelatte, Bleu de Bresse or Pipo Creme.

Baby spinach and grapefruit salad

Serves 4

5 cups (5 oz/150 g) baby spinach
leaves

2 small grapefruit, peeled and
segmented

4 oz (125 g) silken firm tofu, drained
and cut into ¾-inch (2-cm) dice

3 tablespoons olive oil

2 tablespoons fresh lemon juice

1 tablespoon white wine vinegar

½ teaspoon salt

1 teaspoon sugar

cracked black pepper to taste

⅓ cup (1½ oz/45 g) roasted pine or
macadamia nuts

FOR GARLIC FLAKES

⅓ cup (3 fl oz/90 ml) vegetable or
sunflower oil

3 garlic cloves, thinly sliced

Divide spinach, grapefruit and tofu
among 4 salad plates.

In a screw-top jar, combine oil,
lemon juice, vinegar, salt, sugar and
pepper. Secure lid and shake well to
combine and dissolve sugar.

Pour dressing over salad and
garnish with nuts and garlic flakes.
Serve as an accompaniment to fish or
between courses to refresh the palate.

To make garlic flakes: In a small
saucepan, heat oil over medium heat
and cook garlic slices until golden,
30–60 seconds. Drain on paper
towels.

Beans, Grains and Nuts

Fresh bean and feta salad

Serves 4

1 lb (500 g) fresh beans, preferably a combination of green
and yellow lima (butter) beans
1 teaspoon grainy mustard
2 tablespoons balsamic vinegar
5 tablespoons extra virgin olive oil
freshly ground black pepper to taste
¾ cup (4 oz/125 g) feta cheese, crumbled
⅓ cup (½ oz/15 g) fresh basil leaves

Bring a saucepan of salted water to a boil. Add beans and cook until just
tender-crisp, 2–3 minutes. Drain beans and refresh in a bowl of ice water.
Drain again, then pat beans dry with paper towels.

Place beans in a bowl, cover and refrigerate until ready to serve.

Place mustard, vinegar, olive oil and plenty of pepper in a screw-top jar and
shake until well combined. Pour dressing over beans and toss until beans are
thoroughly coated.

Arrange beans on a serving plate and top with feta cheese and basil leaves.

Nutty wholewheat salad

Serves 4
2 cups (8 oz/250 g) cooked wholewheat grain
¾ cup (4 oz/125 g) salted cashew nuts
2 tablespoons peanut oil
2 cups (16 oz/500 g) cottage cheese
½ small cucumber, cut into small cubes
1 bunch scallions (shallots/spring onions), sliced
salt and freshly ground black pepper
1 tablespoon chopped fresh chives, for serving

Mix together wholewheat grain, cashew nuts and oil. Arrange in a ring on a round serving platter.

Combine cottage cheese, cucumber and scallions, and season to taste.

Fill center of wholewheat ring with cottage cheese mixture.

Serve sprinkled with chopped chives.

NOTE Wholewheat grain needs to be prepared in advance. Soak 1 cup (4 oz/125 g) uncooked grain in cold water to cover for 2–3 hours. Cook in boiling water until tender, about 30 minutes. Drain well then let stand until cold.

Couscous salad

Serves 4

1¼ lb (625 g) sweet potatoes or yams (kumara), peeled and cut into 1-inch (2.5-cm) cubes

3 zucchini (courgettes), cut into 1-inch (2.5-cm) slices

3 cloves garlic, finely chopped

sea salt

3 tablespoons olive oil

1 cup (8 fl oz/250 ml) chicken stock

1 cup (6 oz/180 g) instant couscous

3 tablespoons chopped fresh mint leaves

2 tablespoons chopped fresh flat-leaf (Italian) parsley leaves

8 cherry tomatoes, quartered

FOR DRESSING

3 tablespoons lemon juice

3 tablespoons olive oil

sea salt and freshly ground black pepper to taste

Preheat oven to 400°F (200°C/Gas 6). Grease or line a baking pan with parchment (baking) paper. Arrange sweet potato and zucchini in a single layer in pan. Sprinkle with garlic and sea salt. Drizzle with olive oil.

Bake vegetables until golden and tender, 20–25 minutes, turning at least twice during cooking. Remove from oven and set aside.

In a medium-sized saucepan over high heat, bring stock to a boil. Place couscous in a heatproof bowl and add boiling stock. Stir with a fork, cover and let stand until all liquid has been absorbed. Stir again to separate grains.

In a large bowl, combine warm couscous and roasted vegetables with mint, parsley and tomatoes.

To make dressing: Place ingredients in a screw-top jar and shake to mix.

Pour dressing over salad. Toss to combine. Adjust seasoning with salt and pepper. Serve warm, or refrigerate in an airtight container for 1–2 days.

Tabouleh

Serves 4–6

1¾ cups (10 oz/300 g) bulgur/burghul
1 bunch scallions (shallots/spring onions), finely chopped
1 bunch parsley, finely chopped
1 bunch mint, finely chopped
juice of 1 lemon
⅔ cup (5 fl oz/150 ml) olive oil
salt and freshly ground black pepper
1 medium tomato, diced
¼ small cucumber, sliced, for serving
1 onion, sliced, for serving
fresh mint sprigs, for garnish (optional)

Place bulgur in a bowl and cover with cold water. Let stand for 30 minutes.
Drain well, squeezing out as much water as possible.

Return bulgur to bowl and add scallions, parsley, mint, lemon juice, olive oil,
salt and pepper and mix thoroughly. Stir in diced tomatoes.

Turn out into a serving dish. Serve cucumber and onion rings alongside and
garnish with mint sprigs, if desired.

NOTE This salad can be prepared up to 2 days in advance to allow the bulgur to
absorb all the flavors. Keep covered and chilled. Do not add tomatoes until just
before serving.

Kidney bean, beet and red cabbage salad

Serves 5–6
one 1 lb (500 g) can red kidney beans, drained
6 oz (180 g) cooked beets (beetroot), peeled and cubed
6 oz (180 g) red cabbage, shredded
3 tablespoons vegetable oil
1 tablespoon tarragon vinegar
1 teaspoon ground cumin
salt and freshly ground black pepper
1 small radicchio or other red-leaved lettuce
1 small red onion, sliced

Combine beans, beets and red cabbage in a bowl. Add oil, vinegar, cumin, salt and pepper. Mix well.

Line a shallow glass bowl with radicchio leaves. Pile salad in center. Top with red onion slices.

NOTE This salad is especially good if prepared in advance to allow the flavors to develop. Do not prepare lettuce until just before serving.

Rice salad

Serves 2–4

1¼ cups (8 oz/250 g) long-grain white or brown rice
double quantity Vinaigrette Dressing (see page 61)
1 red onion
2–3 stalks celery
4–6 radishes
8–10 black olives, pitted
8–10 cherry tomatoes
4 tablespoons chopped fresh parsley
lettuce leaves, for serving

Cook rice in a large saucepan of lightly salted boiling water until tender but still slightly firm to the bite. Drain well. (If using pasta, rinse under cold running water and drain again.) Transfer to a salad bowl.

Prepare vinaigrette and combine with rice or pasta.

Peel and thinly slice or finely chop onion. Trim and slice celery and radishes. Halve or thickly slice olives and tomatoes. Add vegetables and chopped parsley to bowl. Toss lightly, cover and refrigerate for 1–2 hours.

To serve, arrange lettuce in a shallow serving plate or bowl and spoon rice salad over.

NOTE Substitute small pasta shapes such as penne, spirals, elbows or shells for the rice.

For a main course salad, add any of the following before serving: diced or slivered cooked ham or chicken, drained can of tuna in brine, sliced hard-cooked (boiled) eggs, or toasted pine nuts, walnuts or pecans.

A little fruit is also delicious in a rice salad: golden raisins (sultanas), chopped dried apricots, canned pineapple pieces, fresh orange segments, or diced unpeeled apple.

Pistachio, celery and cucumber salad

Serves 4–6

¼ cup (2 fl oz/60 ml) orange juice

2 tablespoons lemon juice

⅓ cup (3 fl oz/90 ml) extra virgin olive oil

sea salt

freshly ground black pepper

½ red onion, finely sliced into half-moons

⅓ cup (1½ oz/45 g) pistachios, coarsely chopped

4 large celery stalks, finely sliced on the diagonal

2 English (hothouse) cucumbers, peeled and cut into chunks

8 dates, pitted and chopped

¼ cup (¼ oz/7 g) snipped chives

In a large bowl, mix orange and lemon juices with olive oil and season to taste with salt and pepper. Rinse onions under cold water, drain, then pat dry. Add to dressing along with pistachios, celery, cucumber and dates, and mix well. Transfer salad to serving plates, sprinkle with chives and serve immediately.

VARIATION For a lighter version, replace dates with 12–14 seedless red grapes, halved.

Mixed bean salad

Serves 4–6
1 cup (6 oz/180 g) canned chickpeas (garbanzo beans)
1 cup (6 oz/180 g) canned black-eyed peas (beans)
1 cup (6 oz/180 g) canned flageolet or small green lima beans
½ cup (4 oz/125 g) carrots cut into thin strips
1 small red bell pepper (capsicum), cut into thin strips
1 small onion, finely chopped
1 clove garlic, crushed
1 tablespoon cider vinegar
2 tablespoons vegetable oil
½ teaspoon dried tarragon
salt and freshly ground black pepper

Mix chickpeas, black-eyed peas, flageolet beans, carrots and bell pepper together in a large bowl.

Mix onion and garlic with vinegar, oil, tarragon, salt and pepper. Pour onto beans and vegetables and mix thoroughly.

NOTE Any other canned beans could be used, as long as the total weight is kept. Alternatively, try substituting one of the canned beans with an equal amount of lightly cooked fresh green beans.

Seafood

Crab and lime salad

Serves 6

3 tablespoons fresh lime juice

2 tablespoons coconut vinegar (available from Asian markets) or white vinegar

1 teaspoon Asian sesame oil

1 tablespoon olive oil

2 teaspoons fish sauce

1 lb (500 g) fresh or canned crabmeat, well drained

1 fresh small red chili, seeded and thinly sliced

6 scallions (shallots/spring onions), sliced

2 tablespoons chopped fresh cilantro (fresh coriander)

3 fresh kaffir lime leaves, finely shredded, or 1 teaspoon grated lime zest

¼ cup (1½ oz/45 g) shaved fresh coconut, cut into fine strips

¼ small English (hothouse) cucumber, seeded and thinly sliced

2 tablespoons chopped fresh Vietnamese mint

12 fresh betel leaves, for serving (optional)

6 lime wedges, for serving

Place lime juice, vinegar, sesame oil, olive oil and fish sauce in a screw-top jar. Shake to combine and set aside.

In a bowl, combine crabmeat, chili, scallions, cilantro, lime leaves or zest, coconut, cucumber and mint. Add dressing and gently mix until well combined. Place 2 betel leaves, if using, on each plate. Spoon salad onto leaves. Serve with lime wedges.

Tuna and pasta salad

Serves 4

8 oz (250 g) dried pasta shells
salt
one 7-oz (220-g) can tuna in oil
1 bunch scallions (shallots/spring
**   onions), sliced**
1 red bell pepper (capsicum), sliced
¾ cup (4 oz/125 g) sweetcorn kernels
juice of 1 lemon
3–4 tablespoons Mayonnaise
**   (see page 61)**
freshly ground black pepper

Cook pasta in salted boiling water for 8–10 minutes until just cooked. Drain well then transfer to a large bowl.

Pour oil from tuna onto pasta, mix well then let stand until cold.

Add remaining ingredients to bowl, mixing well.

NOTE Preparing this salad up to 1 day in advance allows the flavors to develop. Any other pasta shapes could be used, or use leftover spaghetti or macaroni for a quickly prepared meal.

Crab and artichoke salad

Serves 4

2 cups (8 oz/250 g) white crab meat,
**   fresh, frozen or canned**
6–7 canned artichoke bases, quartered
½ cucumber, cubed
12 radishes, halved
2 tablespoons crème fraîche
1 tablespoon grapefruit juice
salt and freshly ground black pepper
bunch watercress
2 pink-fleshed grapefruit

Place crab meat in a bowl, add artichoke bases, cucumber and radishes.

Beat crème fraîche until thick; add grapefruit juice, salt and pepper. Add to crab mixture, mixing gently but thoroughly. Arrange watercress around edge of a shallow dish. Place crab salad in center.

Peel and segment grapefruit, removing all white pith. Place grapefruit segments in a circle on top of crab salad.

NOTE Always pick over crab meat, whether fresh, frozen or canned, in case any small fragments of shell remain.

Tuna and onion salad

Serves 4

DRESSING

1 fresh small red chili, seeded,
if desired, and thinly sliced,
or 1 teaspoon chili sauce
1 clove garlic, crushed
grated zest of 1 lime
1 tablespoon lime juice
2 tablespoons olive oil
1 tablespoon balsamic vinegar

SALAD

6½ oz (200 g) noodles, e.g. rice stick,
somen, udon or soba
6 oz (180 g) canned tuna in oil, drained
and flaked
1 red onion, chopped
¼ cup (⅓ oz/10 g) chopped fresh
cilantro (fresh coriander)

To make dressing: Place chili, garlic, lime zest and juice, olive oil and vinegar in a screw-top jar. Shake well and set aside.

To make salad: Cook noodles as directed on package. Drain and let cool.

In a bowl, combine noodles, tuna, onion and cilantro. Mix well.

Add dressing and toss until well combined. Cover and refrigerate for 30 minutes to blend flavors.

Spoon into individual bowls and serve chilled.

Grilled shrimp salad

Serves 4

24 raw jumbo shrimp (green king prawns), peeled and deveined, leaving tails intact
2 tablespoons peanut oil
¾ oz (25 g) cellophane noodles
½ green papaya, skinned and cut into matchstick lengths
1 mango, skinned and cut into matchstick lengths
1 cup (1 oz/30 g) loosely packed fresh cilantro (fresh coriander) leaves
½ cup (½ oz/15 g) loosely packed fresh basil leaves
¼ cup (¾ oz/25 g) sliced scallions (shallots/spring onions)

FOR DRESSING
1 fresh small chili, seeded and finely chopped
3 tablespoons fish sauce
4 tablespoons lime juice
1 teaspoon sesame oil
2 teaspoons grated ginger
1 teaspoon shaved palm sugar or brown sugar

To make dressing: Place all ingredients in a screw-top jar and shake well to mix.

Brush shrimp with oil. Preheat a grill pan or barbecue and grill shrimp until they change color, 3–4 minutes, turning during cooking. Remove from grill and set aside.

Place noodles in a heatproof bowl, pour in boiling water to cover and let stand until noodles soften, about 10 minutes. Drain and, using scissors, roughly cut noodles into shorter lengths.

Combine noodles, shrimp, papaya, mango, cilantro, basil and scallions in a mixing bowl. Add dressing and toss until well combined. Serve at room temperature or chilled.

Smoked salmon and avocado salad

Serves 4
4 oz (125 g) smoked salmon, cut into strips
4 celery stalks, sliced
1 bunch scallions (shallots/spring onions), sliced
4 ripe avocados
2 tablespoons lemon juice
2 tablespoons Mayonnaise (see page 61)
2 tablespoons sour cream
1 teaspoon tomato ketchup
few drops Tabasco sauce
salt and freshly ground black pepper
¼ cup (1 oz/30 g) toasted flaked almonds

Place smoked salmon in a bowl with celery and scallions.

Cut avocados in half, discard pits. Remove flesh from avocado using a teaspoon. Reserve avocado skins.

Add avocado flesh to bowl with lemon juice. Mix gently with salmon and celery then spoon mixture back into avocado skins.

Mix together mayonnaise, sour cream, ketchup and Tabasco, taste and adjust seasoning. Spread over top of avocados.

Sprinkle with flaked almonds and serve immediately.

Smoked trout and chili salad

Serves 4

⅓ cup (1½ oz/45 g) unsweetened dried (desiccated)
shredded coconut

¾ cup (6 fl oz/180 ml) water

1½ teaspoons sambal oelek

4 scallions (shallots/spring onions), sliced

1 clove garlic, chopped

⅓ cup (3 fl oz/90 ml) fresh lime juice

10 oz (300 g) smoked rainbow trout, coarsely chopped

2 cups (2 oz/60 g) bean sprouts

1 cup (1 oz/30 g) baby arugula (rocket) leaves, chopped

In a small saucepan over medium heat, combine coconut, water, sambal oelek, scallions and garlic. Bring to a boil, stirring, and cook for 2 minutes.

Remove from heat and let cool completely. Stir in lime juice. Chill until ready to serve.

In a bowl, combine trout, bean sprouts and arugula. Fold in coconut mixture. Serve chilled.

Meat and Poultry

Thai beef salad

Serves 4–6

½ lb (250 g) beef tenderloin (fillet) or sirloin (rump), trimmed, or cooked roast beef

salt and freshly ground pepper

1 tablespoon vegetable oil

⅓ cup (3 fl oz/90 ml) fish sauce

½ cup (4 fl oz/125 ml) fresh lime juice

about 25 fresh small green and red chilies, coarsely chopped

1 teaspoon palm sugar

1 cucumber

1 firm tomato

3 tablespoons thinly sliced shallots (French shallots), preferably pink

½ cup (2 oz/60 g) coarsely chopped celery

5 scallions (shallots/spring onions), cut into 1-inch (2.5-cm) pieces, including green parts

If using raw beef, cut into 1 or 2 thick steaks. Season lightly with salt and pepper. In a large frying pan over medium–high heat, heat oil and cook steaks for a total of 7 minutes per 1-inch (2.5-cm) thickness, turning once, for medium rare. Remove from heat and let cool thoroughly.

In a small bowl, combine fish sauce, lime juice, chilies and sugar. Stir until sugar is dissolved. Cut cucumber in half lengthwise, remove seeds with a spoon if desired, then cut into thin crescents. Core tomato, cut in half vertically, and slice into thin half-moons. Cut cooked meat into thin strips, then toss with fish sauce mixture. Add cucumber, tomato, shallots, celery and scallions, and toss to coat.

Transfer to serving dish and serve immediately.

NOTE Tender beef, such as tenderloin (fillet) or sirloin (rump), is best for this recipe. This is also a good way to use leftover roast beef. For a less spicy salad, leave the chilies whole and lightly bruise them before adding. Although not traditional, this salad is delicious served on a bed of greens, such as green oak leaf lettuce.

Beef salad

Serves 4

1½ lb (750 g) sirloin (rump) steak, in one thick piece, or cooked beef roast

leaves of 1 romaine (cos) lettuce

1 bunch scallions (shallots/spring onions), cut into strips

4 tablespoons olive oil

2 tablespoons red wine vinegar

½ teaspoon black peppercorns, roughly crushed

1 teaspoon chopped fresh tarragon

1 tablespoon chopped fresh mint

1 tablespoon chopped fresh parsley

1 teaspoon Dijon mustard

salt

Remove any fat from steak. Broil (grill) for 3–6 minutes each side, depending on how you like your steak cooked.

Arrange lettuce leaves at each end of an oval serving platter. Sprinkle scallions over top.

Beat olive oil and vinegar together in a large bowl. Add peppercorns, herbs, mustard and salt.

When steak is cooked, cut into thin strips, add to herb dressing then let stand until cold. Transfer to center of platter.

Beef salad niçoise

Serves 4–6

3 tablespoons olive oil
1 onion, chopped
1 clove garlic, crushed
2 cups (8 oz/250 g) cubed eggplant
(aubergine)
1 large green bell pepper (capsicum),
chopped
2 cups (8 oz/250 g) sliced zucchini
(courgettes)

2 cups (1 lb/500 g) skinned, seeded
and chopped tomatoes
1 teaspoon dried basil
1 tablespoon red wine vinegar
salt and freshly ground black pepper
8–12 slices rare roast beef
12 black olives

Heat oil in a large pan, add onion, garlic and eggplant. Cover pan and cook until soft.

Add bell pepper, zucchini, tomatoes and basil, and cook uncovered for about 10 minutes, stirring occasionally.

Remove from heat, let stand until cold, then stir in vinegar, salt and pepper.

Lay overlapping slices of beef on an oval serving dish and spoon cold vegetables around the edge.

Arrange olives on top of vegetables.

NOTE The vegetables can be cooked up to 1 day in advance. Keep covered in the refrigerator. Assemble the dish just before serving.

Vietnamese chicken salad

Serves 6

1 lb (500 g) boneless, skinless chicken thighs and/or breasts, or about 3 cups (1 lb 2 oz/550 g) coarsely shredded cooked chicken, bones and skin removed

about 3 cups (24 fl oz/750 ml) water or stock for cooking chicken, if required

2 cups (8 oz/250 g) bean sprouts, rinsed and drained

leaves from ½ bunch Vietnamese mint

3 fresh long red chilies, seeded and coarsely chopped

juice of 3 limes, freshly squeezed

1 teaspoon salt

½ teaspoon ground pepper

chilies, for garnish (optional)

FOR PICKLED ONIONS

1 lb (500 g) pearl onions or small boiling onions (pickling onions)

1 tablespoon rice vinegar or distilled white vinegar

1 teaspoon sugar

2 tablespoons fish sauce

To make pickled onions: Plunge pearl onions into boiling water, then drain and slip off the skins. If using pickling onions, peel and quarter. In a medium bowl, combine vinegar, sugar and fish sauce. Add onion and let stand for 10–15 minutes.

If using raw chicken, bring water or stock to a boil in a medium saucepan and add chicken. Immediately reduce heat to a low simmer and cook chicken until opaque throughout, 5–7 minutes. Transfer to a plate and let cool. Shred with your fingers or 2 forks into coarse long shreds. Set aside.

Plunge sprouts in a pot of boiling water, then drain immediately and refresh in cold water. Roll several Vietnamese mint leaves at a time into a tight bundle and cut into thin crosswise slices. Repeat to shred all leaves.

At the last moment, in a bowl, toss together onions and their marinade, chicken, bean sprouts, Vietnamese mint and chilies. Season with lime juice, salt and pepper. If desired, garnish with chilies.

NOTE Jars of prepared sweet pickled leeks (cu kieu) are available in Vietnamese and some Asian markets. These are time-saving; use in place of pickled onions in this recipe.

Thai ground chicken salad

Serves 4–6

2 tablespoons sticky (glutinous) rice

2 thin slices fresh galangal

12 oz (375 g) ground (minced) chicken breast meat

2 tablespoons thinly sliced shallots (French shallots), preferably pink

3 tablespoons fish sauce

2 tablespoons fresh lime juice

2–3 teaspoons chili powder, to taste

1 tablespoon coarsely chopped fresh cilantro (fresh coriander) leaves and stems

1 scallion (shallot/spring onion), including green part, coarsely chopped

1 tablespoon coarsely chopped fresh mint

In a wok or small frying pan over low–medium heat, stir rice until golden brown, 3–5 minutes. Transfer to a mortar and pound to a coarse powder with a pestle. Transfer to a bowl and set aside. Pound galangal in the mortar until pulverized.

In a medium bowl, combine ground chicken, galangal, shallots, fish sauce, lime juice and chili powder to taste; mix thoroughly. Heat a wok or large, heavy frying pan over medium heat and add chicken mixture all at once, stirring vigorously to keep it from sticking into lumps. Cook until opaque throughout, about 5 minutes. Transfer to a bowl and let cool slightly, then toss with ground rice and all remaining ingredients. If desired, garnish with additional mint leaves, and accompany with vegetable crudités, such as cabbage, carrot, cucumber and long beans.

Smoked chicken and celery root salad

Serves 4

1 cup (3 oz/90 g) shredded celery root (celeriac)

1 cup (3 oz/90 g) shredded red cabbage

1 small red onion, shredded

1 small green apple, unpeeled, grated

⅓ cup (1½ oz/45 g) coarsely chopped walnuts

2 tablespoons finely chopped fresh mint

13 oz (400 g) sliced smoked chicken

FOR MUSTARD SEED DRESSING

4 oz (125 g) soft or silken tofu, drained

1½ tablespoons fresh lemon juice

2½ tablespoons mustard seed oil or light olive oil

¼ cup (2 oz/60 g) plain (natural) yogurt

½ teaspoon dry mustard

¼ teaspoon cracked black pepper

To make mustard seed dressing: In a food processor, process tofu until smooth and creamy. Add remaining ingredients and process until well combined.

In a large bowl, combine celery root, cabbage, onion and apple. Add walnuts and mint, reserving some of each for garnish.

Pour dressing over salad and toss to combine. Serve with sliced chicken, garnished with reserved walnuts and mint.

Dressings

Dressings are easy to make and add taste and interest to a salad. Endless combinations can be made by varying the ingredients of a basic vinaigrette dressing, using different types of oil or vinegar and adding garlic, mustard or herbs. Extra virgin olive oil is the best quality olive oil but light sunflower or vegetable oils are popular, and good grapeseed, sesame and nut oils are available.

There are fine wine, fruit and herb vinegars on the market and many different mustards and peppers, so experiment with different combinations. Balsamic and sherry vinegars are available from large supermarkets and specialty food stores and give a wonderful aromatic flavor to dishes.

Other dressings are based on mayonnaise or yogurt, citrus juice or Asian-style ingredients such as soy or fish sauce. Select a mix of ingredients that complement the salad. For example, fresh cilantro (coriander) and lime juice go well with the subtle flavor of fish and seafood. For quick and easy dressings, place ingredients into a screw-top jar, shake to mix, then drizzle over salad.

Making Vinaigrette

Generally, the ratio of vinegar to oil is one part vinegar to three parts oil.

1 clove garlic

1 teaspoon Dijon mustard

pinch of sugar

freshly ground black pepper

1 tablespoon white or red wine vinegar or lemon juice

¼–⅓ cup (2–3 fl oz/60–90 ml) virgin olive oil

Peel and halve garlic. Place all ingredients in a screw-top jar. Cover and shake until blended. Or, whisk together all ingredients except oil in a small bowl; gradually add oil, whisking constantly, until dressing thickens slightly. Stand dressing at room temperature to develop flavors, while preparing salad ingredients. Remove garlic and shake or whisk again before serving.

BASIC VINAIGRETTE
6 tablespoons sunflower or olive oil
2 tablespoons white wine vinegar
1 teaspoon superfine (caster) sugar
salt and freshly ground black pepper

BALSAMIC DRESSING
2 teaspoons balsamic vinegar
2 tablespoons olive oil
½ teaspoon Dijon mustard
1 small clove garlic, minced
salt and freshly ground pepper

LIME CHILI DRESSING
¼ cup (2 fl oz/60 ml) fresh lime juice
2 teaspoons grated fresh ginger
1 fresh Thai red chili, seeded and
  sliced
1 tablespoon Asian sesame oil
2½ tablespoons mirin

SOY GINGER DRESSING
2 tablespoons soy sauce
2 teaspoons rice vinegar
2 tablespoons Asian sesame oil
1 teaspoon finely grated fresh ginger

THAI DRESSING
1 tablespoon fresh lime juice
1 tablespoon fish sauce
1 clove garlic, crushed
2 teaspoons shaved palm sugar

SOUR CREAM DRESSING
1 tablespoon white wine vinegar
2 tablespoons olive oil
2 tablespoons sour cream
1 teaspoon Dijon mustard
1 clove garlic, minced
salt and freshly ground pepper

HONEY MUSTARD DRESSING
¼ cup (2 fl oz/60 ml) honey
½ teaspoon salt
 2 tablespoons cidar vinegar
1 tablespoon prepared mustard
1 tablespoon finely chopped onions
¼ cup (2 fl oz/60 ml) water
½ cup (4 fl oz/125 ml) oil

MAYONNAISE
1 egg yolk
1 teaspoon white wine vinegar
salt and white pepper
⅔ cup (5 fl oz/150 ml) sunflower oil

Put egg yolk into a bowl, add vinegar, salt and pepper. Beat until mixed, then add oil, starting with a drop at a time, beating constantly until mayonnaise becomes thick. As mayonnaise thickens, oil can be added in a steady steam. Taste and adjust seasoning. Keep covered and refrigerated, and use within two days.

Index

....

INDEX

A LANSDOWNE BOOK

First published by Apple Press in the UK in 2006
Sheridan House
4th Floor
114 Western Road
Hove
East Sussex BN3 1DD
United Kingdom

www.apple-press.com

Created and produced by Lansdowne Publishing Pty Ltd
Sydney, Australia
www.lansdownepublishing.com.au

Text: Katharine Blakemore
Additional recipes: Vicki Liley, Lynelle Scott-Aitken, Robert Carmack, Deborah Nixon.
With thanks to Tess Mallos for Village Salad and Tomato Salad, page 31.
Photographers: Andrew Elton, Andre Martin, Amanda McLauchlin
Designer: Avril Makula
Production: Sally Stokes
Jacket design: Jane Waterhouse

ISBN-10: 1 84543 124 3
ISBN-13: 978 1 84543 124 2

Set in Trade Gothic and Journal Text on QuarkXPress
Printed in Singapore by Tien Wah Press

Cover picture: Thai beef salad, page 53
Pictured on page 2: Smoked trout and chili salad, page 51
Pictured on page 4: Baby spinach and grapefruit salad, page 33